MEASURE IT!

Measuring Temperature

By T. H. Baer

Gareth Stevens
PUBLISHING

Please visit our website, www.garethstevens.com. For a free color catalog of all our high-quality books, call toll free 1-800-542-2595 or fax 1-877-542-2596.

Library of Congress Cataloging-in-Publication Data

Baer, T. H., author.
 Measuring temperature / T.H. Baer.
    pages cm. — (Measure it!)
 Includes bibliographical references and index.
 ISBN 978-1-4824-3868-0 (pbk.)
 ISBN 978-1-4824-3869-7 (6 pack)
 ISBN 978-1-4824-3870-3 (library binding)
 1. Temperature measurements—Juvenile literature. I. Title.
 QC271.4.B34 2016
 536'.50287—dc23

                                        2015028840

Published in 2016 by
Gareth Stevens Publishing
111 East 14th Street, Suite 349
New York, NY 10003

Copyright © 2016 Gareth Stevens Publishing

Designer: Laura Bowen
Editor: Ryan Nagelhout

Photo credits: Cover, p. 1 Tim Hawley/Digital Vision/Getty Images; pp. 2–24 (background texture) style_TTT/Shutterstock.com; p. 5 Peopleimages/E+/Getty Images; pp. 7, 11, 13, 15, 17, 19 (thermometer) phoelix/Shutterstock.com; p. 7 (summer scene) Piotr Wawrzyniuk/Shutterstock.com; p. 7 (winter scene) Skreidzeleu/Shutterstock.com; p. 9 Eugene Sergeev/Shutterstock.com; p. 11 (ice) StockHouse/Shutterstock.com; p. 11 (boiling) kukaruka/Shutterstock.com; p. 13 (park) Wisiel/Shutterstock.com; p. 15 (sky) Suppakij1017/Shutterstock.com; p. 17 (ice) SOMMAI/Shutterstock.com; p. 17 (boiling) PhotoAlto/Laurence Mouton/Getty Images; p. 19 (boy and mother) Tetra Images/Getty Images; p. 19 (thermometer) Charles Brutlag/Shutterstock.com; p. 21 Triff/Shutterstock.com.

Printed in the United States of America

CPSIA compliance information: Batch #CW16GS: For further information contact Gareth Stevens, New York, New York at 1-800-542-2595.

Contents

Boldface words appear in the glossary.

What's the Weather?

What's the weather like outside? It's easy to see if it's raining or if the sun is shining. But what does it feel like out there? Is it hot or cold? We need to measure the temperature!

The Tools

The tool we use to measure temperature is called a thermometer. Some thermometers are made of a tube of liquid. The red liquid **expands** when the temperature rises and **contracts** when it falls.

hot

cold

Degrees

We use **units** called **degrees** to measure temperature. Lines on the side of a thermometer mark the number of degrees. You can tell what the temperature is by matching the top of the liquid with the degree marks on the thermometer's side.

This thermometer measures 27 degrees.

Using Fahrenheit

One temperature **scale** is called Fahrenheit (F). It's used in the United States to measure temperature. It was invented by a man named Daniel Gabriel Fahrenheit in the 1700s. Water **freezes** at 32°F. It **boils** at 212°F.

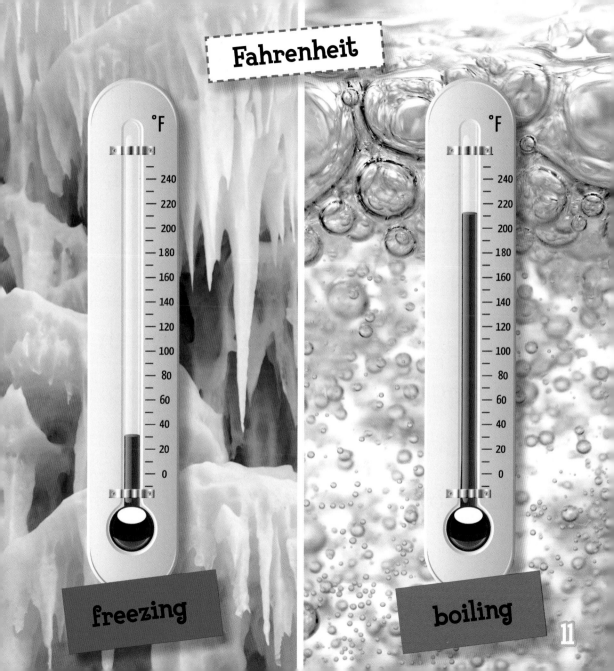

Fahrenheit

freezing

boiling

Let's find out how hot it is outside. This thermometer uses the Fahrenheit scale. Every five lines shows an increase in 10 degrees, which means each line equals 2 degrees. The top of the red line is two marks above 60°. That means it's 64°F!

°F

120

100

80

60

40

20

0

Temperatures often change throughout the day. It often gets much colder when it gets dark. Let's measure the temperature at night. The top of the red line is exactly halfway between 40 and 50 degrees Fahrenheit. Can you tell what temperature it is?

In Celsius

Celsius (C) is used to measure temperature in many other countries. Its scale is based on the temperature at which water freezes and boils. Water freezes at 0°C. It boils at 100°C.

Celsius

freezing

boiling

Converting Temperatures

Celsius can be **converted** to Fahrenheit. Many thermometers have both scales on them so it's easy to convert temperatures quickly. This thermometer says it is 41°F. We can see that equals 5°C.

°C   °F

41°F = 5°C

100.3°F

Average body temperature
is 98.6°F, or 37°C.
A change of just a few
degrees can mean you're
not feeling well!

What About Kelvin?

Scientists use a unit called Kelvin (K) to measure temperature. Zero degrees in Kelvin is called absolute zero, the coldest possible temperature. Scientists use Kelvin because it easily measures very hot and very cold things we find in space!

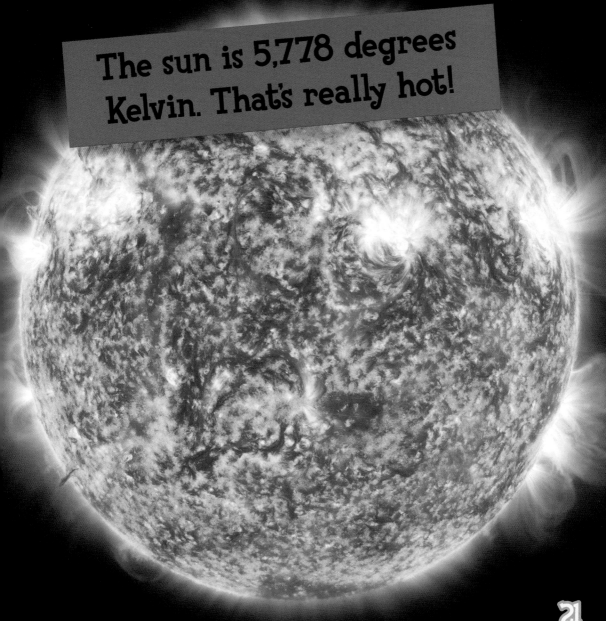

The sun is 5,778 degrees Kelvin. That's really hot!

Glossary

boil: to change from a liquid to a gas

contract: to get smaller

convert: to change from one unit to another

degree: one measure marked on a measuring tool

expand: to get bigger

freeze: to change from a liquid into a solid

scale: a range of values in a standard system for measuring something

unit: a standard amount used for measuring

For More Information

Books

Bailer, Darice. *Measuring Temperature.* Ann Arbor, MI: Cherry Lake Publishing, 2014.

Schuetz, Kristin. *Temperature.* Minneapolis, MN: Bellwether Media, 2016.

Vogel, Julia. *Measuring Temperature.* Mankato, MN: The Child's World, 2013.

Websites

Interactive Thermometer
mathsisfun.com/measure/thermometer.html
This thermometer shows what the temperature is like with certain weather conditions.

Kids Math
ducksters.com/kidsmath/units_of_measurement_glossary.php
Find out more about different units of measurement on this site.

Temperature
weatherwizkids.com/weather-temperature.htm
Learn more about how we measure temperature here.

Index